Dr. Paul's

TOTAL RELIEF

10 Days to a NEW LIFE

Work Book 2

Dr. Paul J. Young

Dr. Paul's
TOTAL Relief
Systems

10 DAYS TO A NEW LIFE

WORK*book* for BOOK 2
Depression

Turbo-Charged Steps To BLAST Your Depression

Dr. Paul J. Young

A **TOTAL RELIEF *SYSTEMS* publication**

DRPAULYOUNG.COM

DEDICATION: This book is dedicated to all readers who finished Book 1, are learning how to unlock the prison doors to their depression and are finding relief. Keep on. The best is yet to come!

All my books are written in a conversational, informal style on purpose. Formality too often bores. I don't want you to get bored while reading this book. I want you to finish it, learn from it and live the truth out in your life. My desire, more than anything, is to help you find TOTAL RELIEF from your depression.

You will find the formatting of the paragraphs and sentences are arranged differently than most other books. This makes it easy to read, easy to get the principles, and most of all will help you, my dear reader, to blast through your depression and find the joy you deserve.

Bravo!

*This book is not intended to replace any kind of therapy you are presently taking. **Always talk with your doctor or therapist** before making any radical changes. And DO NOT stop taking your medication until you have worked through all three books and learned how to apply my unique program. Then, and only then, should you talk with your therapist or doctor to see if you can either stop or reduce your medications.*

In this book I write about many depressed people whom I have counseled. The stories are true but have been disguised enough to protect the identity of those who have overcome their depression. Some stories have been blended with other accounts so that the confidentiality of my true clients can be protected. In all I have worked with thousands who have taken my unique formulas and have found new and transformed lives, for which I am thankful.

INTRODUCTION

A MESSAGE FROM
DR. PAUL

My Dear Reader,

You are reading **WORK***book* 2 in my series of three books that will give you the formulas you need to find TOTAL RELIEF. **This is NOT just another WORK***book* **on depression** and definitely not your typical self-help book as you have found reading Book 1, working through the Workbook and using the Quick Relief YES! Cards.

No way!

You saw in Book 1 and 2, that I take your depression seriously.

But before you continue reading -

STOP!

Have you read Book 1 and 2 in this series?

By now you know that I am not some rookie that doesn't know what I'm doing.

MY APPROACH

My approach to help you goes incredibly beyond what most programs and books offer. In my opinion, almost all texts on depression, even the best sellers, fall short of what you desperately seek. They render some relief, but most of them do not deliver to you the healing and freedom you desire. They do not take you all the way to TOTAL RELIEF.

How many times have you picked up a book or had a therapy session that gave you hope? You experienced some improvement from your depression. But there it is again, raising its ugly head. Your meds aren't working the way they used to, you continue to go to therapy and read books, on and on and on, hoping, to have a break-through. Now you pick up my book. It looks different. You see the title, TOTAL RELIEF.

TOTAL!

That's what you're looking for. Your heart desperately seeks to put your depression behind you…once and for all.

Well, my friend, you have come to the right place.

Teresa needed this help, desperately. I'm sure you recall how her daughter was murdered and the subsequent years of depression that left her in the tank. Think of all she had been through. Who wouldn't get depressed!

My first three formulas helped give her a framework to crawl out of the depression, but she needed more. Then I took her through a few more formulas that you read. It changed her life dramatically.

My promise to you as you work through WORK*book* 2, is this:

You will continue to be taken on a journey that will *not just get rid of your pain, but the ROOT CAUSE of your pain,* restoring you to the person you were meant to be.

Quite a promise, isn't it!

You know now that these formulas work and how your life is already changing because of what you have learned so far.

So work through this Workbook and use the YES! Cards. They will help you to process what you learned in Book 2, and move toward TOTAL RELIEF.

PRACTICE MAKES PERFECT

We all have heard the phrase, "Practice makes perfect." And we all know the truth of that. You can never become good at anything unless you practice.

What I want to do for you in this workbook - and it is called a **WORK***book* on purpose - it is going to make you work. But the work will pay off in big dividends. After all, the goal is to help you find TOTAL RELIEF.

I promise you, if you work this program, you will find a healing that will surprise you. It will change your life in ways that you never thought possible. Some of that change happens as you read BOOK 1, BOOK 2 and BOOK 3. Each book takes you progressively toward that goal of TOTAL RELIEF.

Before you dive into BOOK 3 and do its workbook, you need to learn the lessons of BOOK 2. The old ways of thinking, of interpreting, of acting need to be changed. This doesn't happen overnight. So my suggestion to you, before you move on to BOOK 3, is to work through this workbook, give yourself at least 10 days of practice, learning how to change your thoughts, interpretations and actions.

This 10 day period could bring about the breakthrough you were hoping for and put you on the road to TOTAL healing, BLASTING through the pain of depression.

I will be giving you exercises and assignments that I have often given my clients. These exercises have been proven to help over a number of decades since I have been using them. They will work for you, but only if you PRACTICE them.

Set aside time each day to do this. Put this book on your iPhone or other device and work on it throughout the day. In 10 days you are going to be seeing a new you emerging! It will be fantastic. After you do that, download the Quick Relief YES! Cards. These work like magic in bringing healing to your toxic soul.

Then move on to BOOK 3 and discover three more formulas to break the back of your depression.

I am outlining for you a 10 DAY PLAN to learn these formulas - 10 DAYS to blast through the pain of your depression.

DAY 1

CORE BELIEFS

Let's chart what happens when one has core beliefs and see how they result in our feelings.

BELIEFS	FEELINGS
I am good	Competent
I am bad	Miserable
As a person I am significant	Loved
I'm nobody	Worthless
I can weather any difficulty	Confidence
I am loved (by God and others)	Secure
I belong	Acceptance
No one loves me for who I am	Hopelessness
I am competent	Confidence
I'm a failure	Shame
I'm ugly	Useless
I'm fun to be with	Joy
I can make it through any circumstance	Hopeful
Nothing ever turns out right	Despair
Life is difficult, but I have help from God and others.	Determination

Dig deep and come up with some of your own core beliefs and write what kind of feelings those beliefs are producing. Put this in your journal.

BELIEFS   **FEELINGS**

1.

2.

3.

4.

5.

6.

7.

9.

10.

There are many good and worthwhile core beliefs that can help us break out of depression and find TOTAL RELIEF.

If you believe that you are a person worth loving, and feel that love, it will impact your emotional state. It means that you have thoughts that are rooted, thoughts that interpret reality telling you that you are a person of worth, a person of significance, a person who has value.

List in your journal the reasons why you BELIEVE you are a person:

1. Who is worth loving
2. Who is significant
3. Who is a person of worth
4. Who has great value

If you have doubts - recall Philippians 4:8 and use that passage to focus on the truth, ultimately ending in praise.

End this session by thanking God for WHO YOU ARE. The psalmist said that, "you are fearfully and wonderfully made," (see Psalm 139). Write it in your journal. You might write something like:

1. Thank you God that I am trustworthy
2. Thank you God that I am friendly
3. Thank you God that I have fortitude
4. Thank you God that I am brave
5. Thank you God that I am gentle
6. Thank you God that I am faithful
7. Thank you God that I am adventurous
8. Thank you God that I am easy going
9. Thank you God that I am considerate
10. Thank you God that I am honest
11. Thank you God that I am determined

12. Thank you God that I am humorous
13. Thank you God that I am intelligent
14. Thank you God that I am kind
15. Thank you God that I am loving
16. Thank you God that I am mature
17. Thank you God that I am loyal
18. Thank you God that I am sensitive
19. Thank you God that I am talented
20. Thank you God that I am thoughtful
21. Thank you God that I am wise
22. Thank you God that I am young at heart

GRATITUDE makes us HAPPIER, makes people LIKE US, makes us HEALTHIER, boosts our CAREER, strengthens our EMOTIONS, develops our PERSONALITY, makes us OPTIMISTIC and less SELF-CENTERED, improves our SLEEP, helps us to LIVE LONGER, increases our ENERGY, and brings us closer to GOD.

In EVERYTHING give thanks.

I Thessalonians 5

DAY 2

GOD'S LOVE - A CORE BELIEF

1. Why do you think that believing in God's love is the most important core belief? Write the answer in your journal.

2. What is love? Come up with a general definition. How does God's love differ from human love?

3. Go ahead. Question God's love. Let it all out. Give your reasons why you believe that God does not really love you. List your evidence.

4. Now, put that evidence on trial. Remember Philippians 4:8, in your BOOK 1 WORKbook?   St. Paul said, "Whatever is TRUE." Don't just guess about God's love. Prove it. Come up with at least 20 reasons and proofs that God loves YOU. Write it down in your journal.   If you have difficulty doing this, get a friend to help.

Some time ago, I was speaking about the love of God and decided to take my listeners back before the foundations of the world, into an imaginary room in heaven, the Trinity Room. It is here that all the great decisions are made, including the decision to create human kind and to plan our redemption after the Fall.

This room will not be found in your theological books or in the Catechism. It is not some place that is real. Yet it is real that God made a decision to show his love toward you and me. The reality of this is used in an illustration of the Trinity Room, to emphasize this great point about God's plan to love us, YOU and me, and everyone else.

In this Trinity Room (again, this is an imaginary room - not something we are to believe) the Trinity is in session, God the Father, God the Son and God the Holy Spirit.

The Father speaks:

"Son and Spirit, we have been discussing the last few trillion years or so, this whole project we have, the creation of the world and the making of humankind. We also, in our omniscience know that Adam and Eve will not be obedient but will choose to rebel against our will and follow their own desires. How should we deal with this situation?"

"There are billions of plans we have thought of, all good. But I have come up with what I believe to be the best plan for the recovery and redemption of humankind. I want to share that with you today and see what you think. Whatever we do, we must be in total and absolute agreement."

"What is the plan, Father?" asks the Son. "We are eager to hear your wisdom."

"Yes, Father," the Spirit chimes in. "What is this unique plan that you believe will be the best, the best of billions!"

The Father looks at both of them silently for a moment. In human terms it would have been thousands of years. But for the Trinity, what was time?

Then he spoke.

"I have decided to go to earth to redeem human kind by dying on a cross for their sins… all the sins of the world. Through this, humankind will know for certain that we love them completely and totally."

"You can't do that," said the Son. "I won't think of you going to earth, suffering with sinful humankind and then dying on a cross. It's unthinkable!"

"He's right," piped in the Spirit. "I can see the wisdom of your plan, the desire to show love to the fullest limits, but I cannot agree with this plan. It's not the best. There has to be another plan."

"There is," the Father responded.

For a moment the Father couldn't speak. His eyes clouded up and his voice choked out the words he wanted to say. There was total silence as the Father tried to put into words his thoughts and plan for redemption.

Finally, the Father spoke. "I will not go to earth to redeem humankind. That would not show our love to the full."

"Then what will, Father?" interrupted the Son.

Again the Father choked back the tears. What he wanted to share with his team moved him emotionally. After gaining composure he spoke:

"The best of all plans is not for me to go to planet earth and die for the sins of the world. Instead, the perfect plan that would show our love to the fullest is to (he pauses again for a moment choking back the tears) send YOU my Son, my only Son. There you will suffer and die. There you will experience the full payment for sins, the horrible separation between you and me and the Spirit. It will be awful. The pain that will come into our relationship will be beyond measure."

"What love!"

"But in it, the world will see and be convinced that we love them."

The Father continued: "If I went, that would be great evidence of our love." But if you go, that would be even greater evidence. What father would ever let a son suffer unless it was for love? To give you up when I would rather go, gives humankind the greatest evidence that we love them."

For a moment there was silence in the Trinity Room. Then the Son spoke.

"Father. This is the best of all plans. I know you love me beyond words; an infinite love that could never be questioned. This love of yours toward me and the world will be proved by what I do. Father, I agree to go and suffer, die and redeem humankind, proving to them our love."

"I, too, agree with this plan," the Spirit chimed in. "You are very wise, Father, and this plan is the best plan out of billions of possible plans."

So, back before the foundations of the world, the Trinity made this awesome decision to prove their love toward us.

God proved his love toward us in that while we were sinners, Christ died for us.

Romans 5

5. Did this story give you any more insight into God's love? Write your thoughts in your journal.

6. It is important that you are absolutely convinced that God loves you. If this is not a core belief, you will waiver, often emotionally because of doubts and fears. "How could God allow this to happen to me if he loved me?" you will ask. And your depression will grow deeper and deeper. You must attack these doubts head on. You must "take every thought captive and bring it to the obedience of Christ" (II Corinthians 10).

DON'T BELIEVE YOUR *DOUBTS*

BUT BELIEVE YOUR *BELIEFS.*

Write out now in your journal the evidence you have that God most certainly loves you. Be specific. Dig. Then embrace his love.

DAY 3

WHAT IS KEEPING YOU FROM FULLY EMBRACING GOD'S LOVE?

Chapter 7, in BOOK 2, talks about some reasons that block people from God's love. Let me list some and then you write in your journal what you believe keeps you from embracing God's love the most.

1. **Feelings of unworthiness.** How could God love me for what I have done? Or how could God love me because I am such a bad person.

2. We have a **cloudy view of our forgiveness** and do not really believe that God has forgiven US. He may have forgiven others, but, "Not ME."

3. We have **focused on RULES and not on RELATIONSHIP**. We look at God as demanding, angry, mad if we do not live up to all the requirements of our faith. We have not embraced his love and forgiveness or his patience and understanding.

4. We have a **vending machine view of God**, where God should give us the goodies if we do our part. When this doesn't

happen, we get angry at God. We want it all NOW and are not willing to wait. God will give us sufficient happiness but not infinite happiness until heaven. We don't like that. That anger results in our depression.

5. What are **YOUR REASONS** that keep you from fully embracing God's love? List one or two of the above reasons or others that come to mind.

DAY 4

EMBRACING THE CRUCIFIX

Go to a Catholic Church and spend time in front of the crucifix. This is not just a Catholic thing to do. It is also good for Protestants to do it. Too often the crucifix has been removed from our churches because it is not a pleasant sight - a man suffering, dying.

In our day - we don't want to see suffering. "Get it out of here. I want the resurrected Christ instead."

But there is no resurrection without death. For all eternity, even in heaven, we will be reminded of the crucified Christ, the lamb that was slain (as seen in the book of Revelation).

As you KNEEL before the cross, drink in the agony, the pain, the torture, the horrific separation Jesus felt from his Father. All of this was and is happening for the world...for YOU.

Receive it. Embrace it. Glory in it. Drink it all in.

Then, as you are there, write in your journal what Jesus is saying to you from the cross. Be specific. He wants to tell you something. Listen.

Then spend time in gratitude. Tell Jesus how you feel in your heart, and praise him for his, "unspeakable gift."

DAY 5

THE VALUE OF SUFFERING

We hate pain, don't we? If we can escape it, we feel privileged. We want a life of ease and pleasure. Yet that is not how we grow. That is not how we are shaped into the image of Jesus Christ.

Read Romans 8:28-29. Meditate on it. Grapple with it.

> *All things work together for GOOD for those who love God… that we might be CONFORMED TO THE IMAGE OF CHRIST.*

That's about as clear as you can get…ALL THINGS, all events, all situations. Nothing is left out.

Remember we are like raw diamonds being chiseled. All the raw stuff is taken off. The facets are cut so that we might shine more brilliantly, showing forth the glory of Jesus in our lives. The end product is absolutely glorious.

Spectacular!

But the process is painful.

1. Write down in your journal all the pain you have experienced in your life. Dig deep. Mention it all.

2. Now, knowing that God loved you through the process of your pain, write out what he was trying to do with you, cutting, breaking, polishing.

3. Pause and praise God for the pain. I know that you hate it. But look what it is doing! It is necessary. So smile, and read this personalized writing of Romans 8:28-29.

All things
are working out for the best…
for me.
It is proof that God loves me
and that I love God.
Even the pain that I experience
is God's way of
shaping me,
molding me,
making me
to look and act more like
Jesus Christ.

DAY 6

THE POWER OF
TRUST

The Scriptures say that we should:

*Trust in the Lord with all our hearts and lean not on our
own understanding.*

Proverbs 3:5

Today, focus on this word, trust.

1. What does this have to do with our beliefs and interpretation
    of God's love for us? Write your answers in your journal.

2. How does this impact your feelings?   When you TRUST
    someone, what are you really doing?

3. How will trusting God and his love change your feelings of
    hopelessness?

4. When do you find it easiest to trust God? Hardest?

5. Get into a comfortable chair and picture God's arms around
    you. Totally relax and trust in those arms of love. After all, he
    stretched out those arms on the cross for you.   Let them
    embrace you now. Let all tension go. TRUST.

6. Write in you journal how that felt.

7. Read Proverbs 3:5-6 personalized.

I am going to trust God
with all of my heart,
with all of my mind,
with all of my being.
I choose to not doubt his love,
even though there are things that happen to me
that I do not understand.
Of course I don't understand them.
To do so would make me infinite!
I'm just a finite being,
created by God,
who loves me
and will always do what is best for me.
Because of that, I choose
to trust,
to have confidence in,
to be bold in my assurance
that he is for me,
now and forever.
Amen.

DAY 7

THE POWER OF
PRAISE

In WORKbook 1, we talked about the power of praise using the passage from Philippians 4:8. But I want to help you at this point to understand how praise can blast away your depression almost immediately.

When one chooses to praise instead of condemn, to depreciate, to degrade, life changes and joy returns. And since BOOK 2 is focused on laying a belief in God's love, and proving it to ourselves, then…

**praise of this God who loves us
can be the door
that opens our lives
to that
inner gladness we desire,
that over flowing joy.**

There is a story I want to relate to you before you do some exercises. It's the story of a king who was going being attacked by a great army made up of a coalition of nations who had assembled a mega force to wipe out God's people. There was no way for this king to compete on this battlefield. Failure was assured as this king's kingdom and life were on the line.

Fear swept the land as the people and the king knew that they would be swept away. So they played their ace card. They cried to God. And what happens is one of the craziest strategies in the annals of warfare They knew that without God, a great disaster would take place.

Normally, one would send out the best troops, fierce men who would give their all to defend their homeland, their families, their kingdom. And this King was bent on doing that…until God spoke to him and said:

> *Send out the choir before your great army of fighters. Have them lead the way into battle singing, GIVE THANKS TO THE LORD FOR HIS STEADFAST LOVE ENDURES FOREVER. If you lead the way WITH PRAISE, I will give you the victory. Praise will have the power to overthrow the enemy.*

So it happened. Three nations had gathered to defeat Judah. But they didn't stand a chance when the choir sang praises to God. Instead of fighting Judah, this great army fell into chaos and confusion, and they began to fight each other. By the time the armies of Judah arrived on the battle scene, the great armies that were going to smash them, were destroyed…

Destroyed by praise!

Not a shot fired! Now a sword lifted. PRAISE DID IT ALL!

You can read this true, historical story, in II Chronicles 20, and how king Jehoshaphat overthrew a great army through PRAISE.

Happy the people that know the joyful shout; that walk, O LORD, in the light of Thy face.

Psalm 89:16

PRAISE ALWAYS PREVAILS!

You cannot praise God, clap your hands to him, shout to him with shouts of joy and continue to hold on to your depression.

1. In your journal, write out a list of 500 things you can praise God for. You may think I'm crazy, but this list will be used to blast through all your complaints, all the sad things you choose to focus on rather than ALL THE BLESSINGS God gives to you every day. It will take you more than a day to draw up this list, but work on it day by day. Be determined to develop this great…

Praise list.

It will have the POWER TO BLAST through your moments of depression. The power of praise is an awesome thing!

1) You can focus on **physical blessings**. There are hundreds of physical blessings. For example, you can see (even see in color). Praise him. All your senses are marks of God's blessings (taste, touch, hear, feel, see). You have food in the pantry, a car in the garage. Your mind works, you can walk, and talk. You have heat in the winter and air

conditioning in the summer. You have roads to drive on, grocery stores to shop in. You have clothes in the closet, a washer and dryer, as well as electricity, a computer, a TV, and on and on and on. So many blessings.

2) You can focus on **social blessings** - family, friends, your church

3) You can focus on your spiritual blessings

4) You can focus on the blessings that come from your suffering

2. Sing the song: ***Praise God from Whom All Blessings Flow***

Praise God from whom all blessings flow

Praise HIM all creatures here below

Praise HIM above ye heavenly hosts

Praise Father, Son and Holy Ghost.

A-men

3. Set your watch to buzz every hour. Spend a minute in praise to God. Smile, laugh, clap your hands, shout praises to God. When you do this, you are capturing your THOUGHTS and ACTIONS with praise. You are INTERPRETING your BELIEFS focusing on God's great love to you demonstrated by literally thousands of blessings.

DAY 8

SUFFERING THAT'S REDEMPTIVE

Remember Teresa and what she discovered while kneeling in front of the crucifix? What she learned was one of the MOST IMPORTANT TRUTHS you can ever learn, a truth that will blast you out of the prison of your depression, if you seek to understand it and embrace it.

Let's review what happened.

As Teresa knelt, she felt all the wounds of disappointment and hopelessness that afflicted her, like Thomas, the disciple of Jesus who did not want to believe anymore. He didn't want to have his hopes and dreams dashed again by believing in a resurrected Christ.

"Unless I can touch his wounds, I won't believe," he declared.

Then Jesus appeared and encouraged Thomas to touch the wounds in his hands, feet and side. And it was in the TOUCHING OF HIS WOUNDS that Thomas' faith was renewed. He was changed from a cynical, hopeless man into a fiery apostle of Jesus Christ.

Too many want to bypass the crucified Christ and get on to the resurrection. If they look at the cross, they only want to look at an empty one, not realizing that this Jesus who died for all humankind will bear the wounds of that death…

…forever.

Even in heaven, we will see the Lamb as slain, wounded for us.

It was St. Paul who said to the Philippians:

> *That I may know him, the power of his resurrection AND THE FELLOWSHIP OF HIS SUFFERINGS, being made conformed to his death.*

Now it is true that he put the "power of his resurrection," before the "fellowship of his sufferings." Why? We need that resurrection power to make it THROUGH the suffering. To identify with him, to carry our cross everyday, to be willing to embrace our pain WE MUST have resurrection power flowing through us. When this happens we can face our pain with joy and not just as a stoic, hanging in there gritting our teeth.

St. Paul said in another place:
> *I glory in the cross.* (See Galatians 6:14)

I hate to be a bearer of news that you may not like, but here this: you cannot bypass the cross and embrace the resurrection instead. Why?

Death always proceeds resurrection. There are no shortcuts.

This is why I believe, and it has been proven time and time again in my counseling, that if you fully embrace the cross of Christ, you will then be able to move on into resurrection reality.

THE CROSS IS THE DOORWAY TO THIS NEW LIFE.

That's why, in my counseling I always take people to the cross. It is the turning point, the key that breaks down many of the prison doors of depression and hopelessness.

I call it **REDEMPTIVE THERAPY®.**

It is here at the cross that we enter into the Holy of Holies, that place in God's Temple where the blood of Christ is spilled. The Lamb of God paid the price to LIBERATE us from our sins, our failures, as well as sins against us, intentions meant to harm us and imprison us in hopelessness and depression.

This Holy of Holies is not just a theological position, but an actual place, a place of union with God Almighty, a God who loves you and me and proved it by his sacrifice for us. To find this liberation we must go into the Holy of Holies and embrace Christ's love and let it change us.

Draw me nearer, nearer, nearer blessed Lord
To the cross where thou hast died
Draw me nearer, nearer, nearer blessed Lord
To thy blessed riven side

**If you don't understand HIS WOUNDS,
you won't get over
YOUR WOUNDS.**

**If you don't capture HIS SUFFERING,
you will not gain victory and blast through
YOUR SUFFERING.**

When you see the separation he felt from his father, the horrible pain that he felt, all for us, you will then discover the key to the Christian life.

> *I am crucified with Christ. Nevertheless, I LIVE!*
> St. Paul, Galatians 2:20

Thomas the disciple had to do that. Now Teresa needed to do it.

Teresa, like Thomas, came and knelt before the crucified Christ, all his wounds, all the pain, all his suffering, and peered at him, drinking it all in. As she contemplated his death for her, Teresa became overwhelmed by his sacrifice, his total giving, his love.

Then she broke out in praise and thanksgiving.

> *By his WOUNDS we are healed ...healed in your
> SOULS*
> See Isaiah 53:5, I Peter 2:24

The word "soul" (pseuke in the Greek) found in I Peter 2:24 is the foundation for the word, "psychology." God heals the wounds, our psychological wounds - deep in our souls.

Teresa was discovering this. The light of this truth came flashing through her mind. It was a fresh revelation to her, one that made her thankful for the first time in years.

As she thanked Jesus for all he did for her, a thought suddenly went through her mind that came seemingly from nowhere.

"The Father's Son was murdered just like my daughter was murdered. He knows exactly what I am going through, the pain, the separation, the awful inner torment."

Then she began to sob. God did that for her.

God so loved Teresa
that he gave his only begotten Son
so that if Teresa believes
in Jesus
and embraces his love,
she will not perish,
she will not live out the rest of her life
in the prison of depression,
but instead,
find abundant,
exuberant,
meaningful life

that will never end.

See St. John's Gospel, 3:16

God the Father's son's murder meant life for her. "That horrible death means abundant life for me, NOW!"

Then a thought went through Teresa's mind like a flash of lightening, a thought that started her healing process. She wrote it down so she wouldn't forget it.

"God's murdered son meant life for me. What could my murdered daughter's death mean to others? Could it also bring life?"

When Teresa came back to my office for another session, I could see a change in her already. She was beginning to embrace the love of God in a new way, not just think of it, but know in her heart that it was true. Whatever happened to her, the horrific incident of her daughter's murder could bring about some good.

Wow!

And all of this came about by spending time in front of the crucifix, entering into the Holy of Holies, the place of absolute, pure love and mercy.

When she told me this I rejoiced deeply inside. The core belief about God's love was beginning to impact how she saw life.

1. After reading about Teresa and Thomas the disciple, answer this: What does REDEMPTIVE SUFFERING mean to you? Write the answer in your journal. If you are fighting with how to express it, re-read the passage about Teresa again until you capture not just part of the truth, but the whole of it. It goes deep, deep enough to heal your deepest wounds.

2. It is true, Christ died for you, and all of us. While going through your time of depression, you were suffering. It could be that someone or some event nailed you to a cross. The pain has been horrific. But why did God allow it? Could it be that you are suffering for another person or group of people, that your pain can bring healing to them in ways that you could never imagine?

The story of Joseph, the son of Jacob in the Old Testament, is very instructive here. He had been ridiculed by his brothers and finally sold as a slave, taken to Egypt, and all the good he did seemed to turn bad.

For 13 years he faced harassment and pain. Finally he landed in prison, through no fault of his own, all of this in his 20's and early 30's - the days of his youth, wasting away. And there seemed to be no hope, nothing that would indicate things would change.

Yet Joseph never looked at the outward appearance of events and situations, but knew that his pain, those tortuous 13 years, meant life for others. Joseph said this to his brothers, brothers who were to blame for much of his suffering:

You meant it for evil, but God meant it for GOOD.
Genesis 50

If we could paraphrase Joseph we could say:

All the bad things you and others did to me,
all the suffering I went through for 13years,
all the harassment and struggles I faced,
the heartache,
the loneliness,
the sleepless nights,
the stench in the prison,
the hopes that were constantly dashed,
the false accusations,
the separation from those I loved,
all of this evil GOD MEANT FOR GOOD.
He wanted it to be REDEMPTIVE,
to purify not only me,
but to save YOU my brothers,
who meant all this harm.

Joseph knew that his crucifixion, as it were, meant salvation for those brothers who had hated, ridiculed and despised him.

And in some profound way, there is a deep magic that often occurs when we are open to seeing why we had to go through, or are going through our suffering. This deep magic is simply this; to **embrace the PURPOSE OF OUR PAIN**. That purpose is simply to REDEEM THOSE WHO CAUSED IT, to save them, to see their lives changed.

46

Because of the change in Joseph's brothers brought about by Joseph's suffering, the nations of Israel became great and ultimately produced one of the greatest men of all time, a man who led his people into freedom - MOSES.

What is your pain producing?   Who will it impact if you let it become redemptive, allowing your pain, your personal crucifixion to be given for others?

The world will never be the same!   For the evil done against you WAS ULTIMATELY MEANT FOR GOOD.

> *All things work together for GOOD to those who love*
> *God.*
>   St. Paul

Take the list below and show how your suffering can bring healing for others. This is going to take some work. We hate pain so much that we refuse to see the positive, productive, redemptive side of it. Work on this list now.

You've got cancer.

Your house just burned down.

Your husband had an affair.

Your mother died.

The stock market just crashed.

Someone just smashed your car.

The electricity just went off.

You have a headache.

The divorce is final.

Your child ran away from school.

Your son is on drugs.

A tornado just took off your roof with you in the basement.

Your son is missing in action.

You don't have enough money to pay the bills.

Your knee is swollen.

Your mother just screamed at you.

Your dad molested you.

Christmas shopping again!

You just stubbed your toe.

Your neighbor won't talk to you.

You got bit by a dog.

You're tired.

You have a flat tire.

The dog died.

You have a lot of physical pain.

You weigh too much.

You have no true, close friends.

The boss is angry at you.

You have a tooth ache.

The oven won't work.

The toilet overflowed.

You must have surgery.

Your husband is a jerk.

You are in pain most of the time.

You just gained 5 pounds on vacation.

You can't find a dress that fits.

Your husband is a drunk.

Your feet hurt.

The wind stirs up your allergies.

It's been raining for 5 days.

The blizzard will ruin the Christmas holidays.

The traffic is a mess.

The flight will be 3 hours late.

You are going to die in 3 months.

You faced ridicule.

3. Yes, you have been crucified with Christ and have faced all the shame, the pain, the aloneness, the rejection, all for what? To be a redemptive force in the lives of others. Spend some time now PRAISING GOD for the opportunity to be that redemptive force in the lives of others as you read these verses.

> *Then they left the presence of the council, rejoicing that they were counted worthy to suffer dishonor for the name.*
>
> Acts 5:41

Beloved, do not be surprised at the fiery trial when it comes upon you to test you, as though something strange were happening to you. But rejoice insofar as you share Christ's sufferings, that you may also rejoice and be glad when his glory is revealed.

I Peter 4:12-13

4. As people see you suffer, and in spite of it, they see your joy, they will be amazed by your faith and some, if not many, will be brought to Christ. Who do you think is watching you now? List their names in your journal.

DAY 9

BEHAVIOR THAT
MATCHES YOUR BELIEF

We covered three formulas in BOOK 2.

1. Formula 4:

Belief = Feelings.

It is here that we focused on the core belief of God's love. Once we REALLY BELIEVE and embrace God's love for us, once we have a settled assurance that he is for us and not against us, we will be on the way toward TOTAL RELIEF. Doubt leads to depression, and depression spawns doubt. What is the way out? Kneel before the crucified Christ. Drink in the proof of his love that was then and is forevermore. Then go, knowing that, "Jesus loves me, this I know."

2. Formula 5:

Event + Belief (in God 's love) + Interpretation (in light of God's love) = Feelings of Hope.

It is here that we CHOOSE to interpret every event and situation that happens to us in light of God's love. He is there for us, and often uses the painful times to shape us to be more like Jesus. It is here that we actually embrace our suffering and our pain, because we know that like a grand piece of marble, he is chiseling away, taking away all that doesn't belong there in our lives, so that we might be a glorious statue, a person that shines with beauty and wonder.

When we know what we shall be, we submit to the creator's hand, with joy. And as we bear these sufferings, we realize that it is not just for us, but for others too, a redemptive suffering where our pain brings gain to others.

3.   Formula 6:

Event + Belief + Interpretation + *Behavior* (love) **= Feelings**

Today, DAY 9, we want to focus on your behavior, actions of LOVE. In BOOK 2, we have focused entirely on love - love capturing our BELIEFS and INTERPRETING all things in light of that love. As we do so, our BEHAVIOR changes, for "faith without works is dead." So our works prove that we really believe it is true, that God so loves the world, God so loves me that he GAVE..." God's love is demonstrated, is shown through his behavior of giving. In light of this, here are some things you can do on day 9.

1.   Write out a list of people in your journal who have hurt you that you need first of all to forgive, and to do it in your heart. You need to let go of the resentment, the bitterness, the blaming and say in your heart:

" (name the person) I forgive you, completely and totally. You may have meant it for evil, but God meant it for good. God used you to develop me. So I can't spend my time blaming you for something that may ultimately turn out to be for my good."

2. In I Peter 3, we are told not to curse people who have wronged us, but rather to bless them instead. Write out ways you are going to bless the person or persons who have wronged you. Be specific.

   1) You may send an uplifting card full of hope and cheer and write something like this:

      I hope this finds you well. May God give you all your heart's desires.

      Sign your name

   2) You may bake them a cake or cookies, or give them something you know they would like.

   3) You may call and confess your attitude of blame and ask them to forgive you. Even though they were responsible for the initial action, you are responsible for your reaction of blame and un-forgiveness. Let it go! The weight of it is causing you to be depressed. Release it. Bless them.

   4) Draw up a list of positive traits that you can use to praise this person. Remember Philippians 4:8? We are to focus on things that are "worthy of praise." When you talk or

write this person, use a few of these positive traits in your discussion. It will bring healing to them...AND TO YOU!

5) Pray for this person, not prayers of condemnation, but prayers of blessing. "God bless (name person) and give them everything they need today. May they experience your love and generosity. Amen."

3. Don't forget to love yourself. It is easy to get caught up in shame and remorse for something that we did. All this gets is depression. We must *behave* towards ourselves as Christ did - with forgiveness and blessing. Receive that love, that forgiveness, that blessing. Drink it in. Bless yourself too! Give a gift to yourself. Praise yourself. This is not an act of sinful pride, but of joyful acceptance, believing in a God who loves you deeply and behaving in light of that love.

DAY 10

LAYING PLANS TO SUCCEED

Draw up what you need to do to better put into practice the things you have learned in BOOK 2. Here are some suggestions:

1. Re-read BOOK 2, and write in your journal thoughts that you need to remember and put into practice.

2. Go through the **WORK***book* again and work on those exercises that will help you to change your BELIEFS, INTERPRETATIONS and BEHAVIOR.

3. Constantly remind yourself about redemptive suffering, what it is and how it can impact you and others. Set times you will spend in front of the crucifix, drinking in what Jesus did for you and how your suffering, like his, can bring life to others.

4. Act as a detective and catch yourself when you are interpreting events and situations in such a way that bring depressed feelings, interpretations that do not embrace God's love.

5. Catch yourself when you flip your interpretation and as a result, feel good.

6. Carry your journal and report each day how you are doing with BELIEFS, INTERPRETATIONS AND BEHAVIOR. Pat yourself on the back as you improve.

7. Share what you are learning with someone else. Sharing often helps to deepen the truth in your own life as you embrace it and talk about it with others.

8. List your own plans and what you need to do to embrace the truth you have learned about BELIEFS AND BEHAVIOR and the three formulas in BOOK 2. Write this in your journal. Be specific. The more you work on rewiring your thinking system, the more you will succeed and find TOTAL RELIEF.

CONGRATULATIONS!

Be sure and download the **Quick Relief YES! cards** for Book 2,
You will then be ready to move onto BOOK 3.

In BOOK 3 you will move on to some new surprises as you work
not just to get rid of the pain of depression, but the wounds that
caused that depression in the first place.   You can buy it on
amazon.com.

Pain is not optional…misery is!

Happiness is a choice.   And you are choosing to move into that
circle of full and TOTAL RELIEF, into that circle of absolute,
glorious joy!

Dr. Paul

Education:

University of California, Fresno, B.A in English

Dallas Theological Seminary, Th.M (Masters in Theology)

Biola University, Doctorate of Ministry with emphasis on psychology (working with Talbot School of Theology, Rosemead School of Psychology and other schools)

Dr. Paul Joseph Young helped grow one of the largest churches in the Dallas/Ft. Worth area as its pastor, working with thousands of people, developing his skills both as a minister, communicator and a counselor. For seven years he was C.E.O. of Community Bible Study International, working in over 60 countries of the world.

Dr. Paul's communication skills has made him a favorite speaker around the world. He lives with his wife Diane. They have five children and 14 grandchildren.

More than anything, Dr. Paul lives to help people find the joyful life they deserve.

OTHER BOOKS BY DR. PAUL

1. **Lethal Discord** a Catholic Thriller. This has been called a "page turner" by many who read it. You will live the story and learn about your faith as you read this compelling novel.

2. **Lethal Discord companion guide** with questions that will help you dig deeper into the novel.

3. **Great Men of the Bible - Saint Paul, his secret to success.** The story of his success can be yours!

4. **The Personalized Bible, Philippians**
    This book will help you to make right choices about feeling great. I take the book of Philippians, a book in the New Testament, and write it as if it were written to YOU. Reading this book for 30 DAYS in a row could have a great impact on the joy you experience every day.

5. **Amazing Women of the Bible** - women you never knew before. Read this dramatic presentation of these great women! You will not be the same.

6. **Know What You Believe** - the catechism for today. A simple way to learn what you believe, a method for you and your family can use that will give you a depth of understanding of your Catholic Faith.

7. **You Can Change Your World** - a powerful book that gives us the secret to changing our world. It's explosive!

8. **How To Finish Well.** A Catholic book for Retired men who want to make the most of their retirement.

9. **Potato Salad for the Depressed Soul** - Magical steps to take to blast away depression while making potato salad! This is a crazy book that could change your life and bring the joy you are looking for.

10. **TOTAL RELIEF SYSTEMS SERIES** (3 books in each category - 9 books total). These are books written to help people overcome their emotional struggles and find peace, purpose, and joy. They take a person into an in depth journey to find restoration and healing for their souls.

- **Dr. Paul's TOTAL RELIEF - ** Depression

- There are *NINE books in this series*, books that will liberate you from depression and anxiety, setting you on the pathway toward JOY, the kind of life you dreamed of.

11. **Dr. Paul's FEELING GOOD ToolBox.** There are so many things that happen to us with interpretations that guarantee that we feel bad. Want to change your interpretations and actions so you feel a lot better? This is a must read. It will TRAIN you to think and act right.

12. **The NOTE.** Why has the music left your soul? What is life all about? How can I get music back into your inner being, a song that fills me with hope and joy? This book is both a visual and verbal parable about the NOTE and how he can change you life...NOW!

13. **30 Days To Making Your Wife Feel Special.** This book could radically change your marriage...in only 30 days. Take the challenge. You nor your wife will be the same.

14. **If There Is A God, Whose God Is God?** Who's right, the atheists? The agnostics? What about the eastern religions, or the Jews, or Islam? And then all those Protestants...why do Catholics believe that the Church is really Catholic? Lots of questions. Lots of answers. It will be a faith-building adventure.

15. **The Unexpected Visitor.** What would happen if you opened your front door and saw Jesus standing there, wanting to come in a stay for a few days. What would you do? How would you act? Would you make any changes? This book delves into a couple who had to allow Jesus to stay with them and the changes it made in their lives.

16. **How To Be An IMPACT MAN** - a powerful book that will help men to become spiritual forces in their homes, Churches, workplaces and the world.

   *This book is also published in a young adult edition designed for college student and young single men.

17. **The IMPACT MAN *Daily Walk*** - a daily devotional for men that will take them to another level in their walk with God. It's practical and powerful! (also in a Young Adult edition).

18. **How To Be An IMPACT WOMAN** - a powerful book that will help women to become spiritual forces in their homes, Churches, workplaces and the world.

19. **The IMPACT WOMAN *Daily Walk*.** This daily read includes all the books of the bible from Genesis to Revelation with each day focusing on I.M.P.A.C.T. Reading it every day will revolutionize your life.

20. **GUARANTEED RECOVERY from a loss.** Have you lost something dear, a relative, friend, home, job, reputation or money? This book is for you. I teach a simple T.A.P. technique for overcoming loss and finding peace and joy again.

21. **Gold, Glory & Girls.** What do men want? What do they really want and need? This book takes them on a journey to the forth "G" that men need…GOD and the fulfillment that brings to their souls.

22. **I'm Praying The ROSARY for YOU!** This book will not only change your life as you pray the Rosary but will change the lives of family members and friends you pray for. You not only buy the book for yourself but buy a copy for each person you pray for and send them this personal book with their name written in it over 100 times! When a family member or friend read the prayers you are praying for them, they will, in many cases, be brought closer to God and begin to not only live out their faith, but begin to impact others too.

23. **The Personalized ROSARY.** You will learn how to pray the Rosary in a specific, purposeful, powerful way…just for YOU! Your life will not be the same as you pray these prayers and draw closer to our Blessed Mother and Jesus Christ our Lord.

24. **How To Pray The ROSARY For Your Family.** You can have great impact on your family through your prayers. The Holy Spirit will take what you pray and in obvious and subtle ways make it happen in God's time as you pray specifically with purpose and direction. This book will guide you how to pray POWERFUL PRAYERS for your family, prayers that will not only change them…but you!

25. **How To Be A MIGHTY MAN of GOD.** In this book Dr. Young used the Scripture by St. Paul in I Corinthians 16:13-14 to develop the 5 STEPS that need to be taken to become a mighty man of God. This powerful book will awaken you of your need and move you to take simple steps to become the man you were always meant to be. It is a great book to use for a men's retreat with helps for leaders on how to organize one.

See many other books at DrPaulYoung.com

This is a
TOTAL RELIEF *SYSTEMS*
publication

My prayer for you:

May you break down the prison bars of your depression
May you learn that you don't have to be weighed down
    Heavy
    Bitter
    Hopeless
    Angry
    Resentful
    Alone.
May you experience the fullness of who you were meant to be
    Bold
    Engaged
    Alive
    Filled with happiness
    Overflowing
    With exploding joy!
May God grant you the desires of your heart.

Amen

To help you make great progress, be sure and download my

Dr. Paul's Quick Relief YES! Cards.

You can find them on my website at DrPaulYoung.com

These cards are specific prescriptions that will help you to heal faster - true medicine for the soul. They are worth their weight in gold!

I've also made an appointment to see you in BOOK 3

I am going to take you a lot deeper, drilling down to the foundation of your thoughts so that you can be more affective in interpreting every event that happens to you and come out feeling good.

Dr. Paul's
TOTAL RELIEF
Book 3
DEPRESSION

Covering additional, healing formulas
BREAKTHROUGH formulas that will liberate you
More than you'd ever imagine!

I would appreciate if you would **give me a good review of this book.** A good review (5 stars) encourages people to read the book and hopefully change their lives. Thank you for taking the time to do this. Go to this book title where you bought it at amazon.com.

A DrPaulYoung.com publication

Products that make a difference now…and forever

www.ingramcontent.com/pod-product-compliance
Lightning Source LLC
Chambersburg PA
CBHW072256310526
45795CB00012B/1667